The CALUMET COLLECTION

A HISTORY OF THE CALUMET TROPHIES

———————————

JUDY MARCHMAN AND TOM HALL

———————————

FOREWORD BY MARGARET B. GLASS

ECLIPSE PRESS

Lexington, Kentucky

Library of Congress Control Number: 2001096885

ISBN 1-58150-077-7

Printed in The United States
First Edition: April 2002

Distributed to the trade by
National Book Network
4720-A Boston Way
Lanham, MD 20706
1.800.462.6420

a division of The Blood-Horse, Inc.
PUBLISHERS SINCE 1916

Contents

Foreword .... *page 6*
A Golden Dynasty .... *page 8*
The Glint of Greatness .... *page 12*

CALUMET TROPHIES BY DECADE

1930s .... *page 13*
1940s .... *page 23*
1950s .... *page 61*
1960s .... *page 85*
1970s .... *page 91*

CALUMET HORSE BIOGRAPHIES

Nellie Flag .... *page 14*
Bull Lea .... *page 18*
Whirlaway .... *page 24*
Mar-Kell .... *page 28*
Twilight Tear .... *page 32*
Armed .... *page 40*
Citation .... *page 46*
Wistful .... *page 50*
Coaltown .... *page 54*
Bewitch .... *page 62*
Real Delight .... *page 66*
Two Lea .... *page 70*
A Glitter .... *page 78*
Tim Tam .... *page 82*
Forward Pass .... *page 88*
Our Mims .... *page 94*
Alydar .... *page 98*
Davona Dale .... *page 104*
Before Dawn .... *page 108*

Calumet Honor Roll .... *page 110*
Acknowledgments .... *page 111*

The Wright Way

The fifty golden years of Calumet Farm Thoroughbreds (1932-1982) represent a dynasty that will never be equaled. When Warren Wright Sr. inherited the farm from his father, William Monroe Wright, inventor of Calumet Baking Powder, he proceeded on the theory that horse lovers and racing fans should see what was behind these racehorses — the love, attention, planning, expense, and handling that preceded their feats at the track. He welcomed visitors to the 1,038 acres on Versailles Pike, near Keeneland, and many families came, year after year, considering themselves part of the "Calumet family."

When I was offered the secretary job there in April of 1940, my boss of three and a half months at Southeastern Greyhound Lines said I must take it, as it was the "chance of a lifetime!" I never knew how he knew this in early 1940, but he was so "W-right"!

Whirlaway "put us on the map" in May 1941, winning our first Kentucky Derby and going on to win the Triple Crown. In August of 1941, the Wrights and trainer Ben Jones celebrated "Whirlaway Day" on the farm. Traffic was so heavy that the police were called to control it.

Mr. Wright died on December 28, 1950, leaving Calumet to his wife, Lucille Parker Wright, of Maysville, Kentucky, as owner for her lifetime. On her death on July 24, 1982, the farm passed to Wright's remaining heirs.

In 1952 Lucille Wright remarried, to retired U.S. Naval Reserve Rear Admiral Gene Markey. She wanted the trophies kept in Kentucky forever, but changed her will after Churchill Downs took more than five years to give us the 1968 Forward Pass Derby cup, following Dancer's Image's disqualification. She eventually redirected them to the National Museum of Racing in Saratoga Springs, New York.

In 1979 I realized this would come to pass when "Armageddon hit us" (her death) if something were not done while she was living. Due to her failing health, it was too late for her to change her will again. In February 1980 her Revocable Trust was set up and I was Kentucky Trustee. Meantime, I had enlisted the help of James E. "Ted" Bassett III, then president of Keeneland Association, to help me find a way to keep the trophies in Kentucky. Ted recruited Kentucky Governor John Y. Brown to help. After much negotiating, we all met on June 15, 1982. All the upcoming remaindermen [the remaining heirs], lawyers, trustees, and others involved agreed to sign the papers to place the trophies at the Kentucky Horse Park. By the last weekend that June, the state was ready to arrange the transfer. We had a two-day "assembly line" in the Markey residence on the farm, matching all  the trophies to my inventory cards, having the trophies appraised by Sotheby's, photographed, recorded by the state, and packed to go. Unbelievably three weeks and three days later, we lost Mrs. Markey without warning. Kentucky had come that close to losing the trophies!

In subsequent years the farm, in the hands of the remaindermen, was in bankruptcy. Ted Bassett started a "Save the Calumet Trophies" campaign, resulting in $1.2 million in public support. Finally, the Commonwealth of Kentucky came up with an additional $1.5 million for a total of $2.7 million — and the struggle ended after an odyssey of nearly twenty years, involving legal battles, creditors, appraisers, remaindermen, Kentucky government, trustees, bankers, besides a caring community including Cassidy School children, all "Calumet lovers," who responded to help! The courts ruled that this wonderful collection of gold, silver, crystal, etc. — every conceivable type, shape, and size of trophy — would remain in Kentucky where it belongs — FOREVER! With this resolution, Mrs. Markey is surely resting in peace in the Lexington Cemetery.

Margaret B. Glass
Calumet Farm secretary — 1940 to 1982

A Golden Dynasty

Calumet Farm lies just west of Lexington, Kentucky, on land that rises and falls almost rhythmically. The farm's hundreds of acres of bluegrass nurtured Thoroughbreds whose performances across five decades transformed an idyllic piece of real estate into legend.

Using the Calumet Baking Powder fortune, William Monroe Wright had built Calumet Farm into a successful Standardbred operation, but Warren Wright didn't share his father's same equine passion. He converted Calumet into a Thoroughbred farm.

Wright purchased his first broodmare in 1931, paying $6,100 Depression dollars for Nellie Morse, the last filly to win the Preakness. The large bay mare was in foal to American Flag, a classic-winning son of Man o' War. The resulting foal, a chestnut filly named Nellie Flag, would become Calumet's first champion, first Kentucky Derby starter, and a foundation broodmare.

Wright pursued good fillies and mares from well-established breeders the way a prospector pursued gold nuggets. Soon he had acquired a powerful nucleus of broodmares whose produce would radiate far into the future.

In 1936 he bought a yearling colt by Bull Dog. This colt, Bull Lea, would become a leading sire and the keystone of Calumet's racing fortune.

Once Bull Lea's progeny hit the tracks, the farm garnered titles, one hard upon another. From 1940 through 1949, Calumet Farm was never worse than third in the leading owner category, finishing first in seven of those years. In 1947 Calumet became the first farm to pass the one-million-dollar earnings mark. That year it owned the champion two-year-old colt and filly, the champion handicap horse, and the Horse of the Year. Starting with Whirlaway in 1941, Calumet bred and raced two Triple Crown winners, four Kentucky Derby winners, four Preakness winners, and two Belmont winners. By the end of the forties, the stable had campaigned nine horses responsible for twenty-five championship titles. Citation, Bewitch, Coaltown,

The main gate at Calumet Farm

Twilight Tear, and Whirlaway — horses whose names are forever linked with racing's glory days — plundered racetracks across the country, adding silver and gold to the trophy cases in the Calumet mansion. Calumet was becoming a dynasty to rival that of its predecessors, the powerful stables of the Whitneys, the Maddens, the Dwyer brothers, and the Belmonts.

Fortune continued to hold Calumet in its palm throughout the fifties. Wright died in 1950; the traditions of Calumet did not. His widow, Lucille, assumed the mantle and the legacy. In 1951 Citation became the first horse to earn more than one million dollars. In 1952 Mrs. Wright married Rear Admiral Gene Markey. Calumet once again dominated the leading owner's list: from 1950 through 1959, it led four times and finished second on three occasions. Its horses — Two Lea, Real Delight, Barbizon, Tim Tam — added more championships. The record for number of wins by an owner/breeder in the Kentucky Derby fell, as three more homebred runners wore the devil's red and blue and a blanket of roses in the winner's circle. Two more Preakness trophies stood with the growing collection of Calumet trophies. By this time Calumet had packed in its tack trunk a trophy from almost every major race across the country.

But nothing lasts forever.

The sixties brought a decline. Ben A. Jones, Calumet's trainer/general manager since 1939, retired. His son, H.A. "Jimmy" Jones, followed in 1964. Bull Lea, Calumet's premier sire, was long past prime and had been pensioned. He died in 1964. The farm would relinquish its stranglehold on the top of the leading owner's list. Only once, 1961, would it finish first. There were hints of returns and always hopes, but these remained no more than shadows. There were good horses like On-and-On and Beau Prince, but none great. Only one, Forward Pass, returned Calumet to the headlines of the sports pages and became a reminder of faded glory. He inherited the Kentucky Derby on the disqualification of Dancer's Image, bettered his rival to win the Preakness (Calumet's seventh), and garnered a year-end championship.

The dearth of winners continued throughout the early seventies. When John Veitch became Calumet's trainer in 1976, the stable was at its lowest point since its inception in 1932. It recorded a hapless four wins in the entire year. But the seeds of resurgence were germinating. In addition to the wins, the record shows ten second-place finishes, two of which were stakes-placed finishes by a maiden two-year-old, Our Mims. The following

The Calumet Farm office

The cemetery with Bull Lea's statue presiding

year the bay filly brought Calumet its first Eclipse Award as champion three-year-old filly of 1977. Her half brother Alydar was the second-leading two-year-old colt and on the verge of greatness through his close two-year rivalry with Triple Crown winner Affirmed. Alydar was arguably one of the greatest horses never to win a championship as a racehorse. He would be a leading sire, a rival to Bull Lea's greatness, but that honor came under a different regime and in the final act. Another three-year-old filly champion followed in 1979. Davona Dale's success propelled Calumet to fifth place on the leading owners' list and to back-to-back million-dollar earning years as the decade ended.

The eighties brought a last breath of the past: a two-year-old filly who was Calumet-bred through and through. Before Dawn, in an almost perfect racing season, won the Eclipse Award for leading juvenile filly.

Lucille Wright Markey died in 1982 and with her the Calumet tradition of old.

Glimpses of that tradition are reflected by each piece of silver and gold and crystal in the Calumet trophy collection. Its permanent home at the Kentucky Horse Park is a tribute to the judicious devotion of those who honor the golden age of Calumet Farm.

Nellie Flag

Nellie Flag was the first in a seemingly never-ending line of firsts for Calumet Farm: first homebred stakes winner, first Kentucky Derby starter, first champion.

At two Nellie Flag developed into a strong, vigorous filly of some size and scope. She was also blessed with speed and the body type that suggested she could carry that speed over a distance. On July 18 at Arlington Park in Chicago, Nellie Flag started for the first time. The young Eddie Arcaro, whose career would intertwine with the rising fortunes of Calumet Farm, rode her. She won by three-quarters of a length.

Three gigantic efforts in premier two-year-old races earned her championship honors in 1934. In the Matron Stakes at Belmont Park, Nellie Flag faced the top two-year-old fillies and summarily dispatched them.

Laurel's Selima Stakes presented another opportunity for Nellie Flag to face the best of her class. Despite bearing out in the final furlong, she won by three-quarters of a length.

Nellie Flag returned home for the Kentucky Jockey Club Stakes. Favored, she won by a length and a half. It would not be the only time she would be the favorite in an important race at Churchill Downs.

Spending the winter at Calumet, Nellie Flag filled out her rangy frame. In a prep race on April 27 at Churchill Downs, Nellie Flag flew to the lead and kept unfurling. At the end of the muddy seven furlongs, she was ahead by six lengths, an impressive performance. The 1935 Kentucky Derby was a short week away.

In spring it's not only a young man's fancy that turns to thoughts of love. With seventeen handsome Derby colts all around, biology conspired against her, and her thoughts were not on racing. She was also the unlucky victim of a roughly run race. She did not disgrace herself, finishing fourth to eventual Triple Crown winner Omaha.

Nellie Flag earned a measure of Derby revenge when her great grandson Bold Forbes won the 1976 Kentucky Derby.

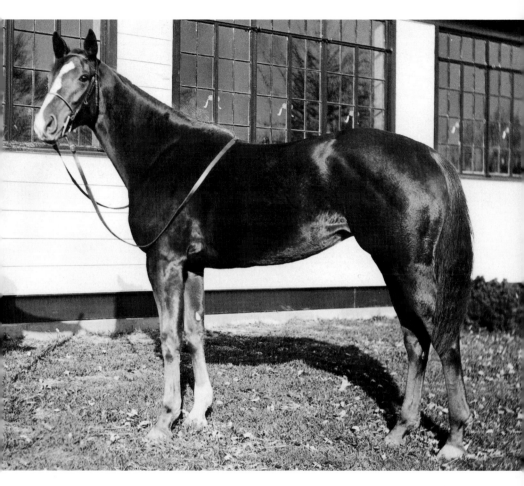

			Fair Play
Nellie Flag 1932 chestnut filly	American Flag	Man o' War	Mahubah
		Lady Comfey	Roi Herode
			Snoot
	Nellie Morse	Luke McLuke	Ultimus
			Midge
		La Venganza	Abercorn
			Colonial

RACE RECORD	STARTS	1ST	2ND	3RD	EARNINGS
(Stakes in Parentheses)	22	6 (3)	5 (2)	1	$59,665

SILVER BOWL

Made by International, this trophy is the first Calumet Farm earned. The Rhode Island governor presented it to Warren Wright. Unlike most Calumet runners, Hadagal was purchased as a yearling for $4,000.

won by:
Hadagal
at Narragansett Park

SILVER URN

The perpetual trophy was made in England by Crichton Brothers of London. William Woodward of Belair Stud donated it in memory of the mare Selima who was imported to Belair in the reign of George II. Nellie Flag was Calumet's first of three winners in the Selima, followed by Miss Keeneland (1943) and Whirl Some (1947). With Whirl Some's victory, Calumet retained possession of the perpetual trophy.

won by:
Nellie Flag
at Laurel Racecourse

SILVER URN

This rare, ornate sterling silver footed urn with cover was made in Augsburg, Germany, in the 17th century. The converted sanctuary lamp stands 22 inches tall. Calumet purchased Crossbow II as a foal beside his dam at Saratoga in 1933.

won by:
Crossbow II
at Saratoga Racecourse

SILVER PITCHER

An 11-inch sterling silver pitcher made by I.I. Cox in New York, circa 1835. With an S-curve handle and beading around the top, this is the first trophy of 20 Calumet won at its hometown racecourse.

won by:
Count Morse
at Keeneland Racecourse

Bull Lea

Neatly tucked in the rear of Calumet Farm is the land set aside as the final resting place for its hallmark horses. Holding pride of place is a statue of Bull Lea, who was the cornerstone of Calumet's success.

At Saratoga in 1936, a strong, good-bodied bay colt, blessed with the presence of the best of his breed, entered the sales ring as property of Coldstream Stud. The son of Bull Dog would leave some fourteen thousand spirited-bid dollars later belonging to Calumet Farm.

Although Bull Lea's record as a sire far overshadowed his performance as a racehorse, to intimate he was a moderate performer on the track would be unjust. His last two performances at two suggested greater potential. He finished second in two major stakes, the Hopeful at Saratoga and the Champagne at Belmont Park.

At three Bull Lea debuted at Keeneland, defeating a field that included Menow, champion two-year-old colt of 1937. Showing speed, Bull Lea led from the start in track-record time. One week later Bull Lea pressed Menow's pace in the Blue Grass Stakes, again winning in track-record time. Nine days later, he finished eighth, as second choice, in the Kentucky Derby. During the year he added three more stakes victories.

Arguably Bull Lea's best race was the 1939 Widener at Hialeah. He defeated Stagehand by two and a half lengths. Later he injured his leg and was sent to the farm.

A strapping 16.2 hands, Bull Lea wasted little time in proving his worth as a stallion. His first crop contained stakes winners Twilight Tear, Armed, Durazna, and Harriet Sue. Three of the four would be champions; two, Horse of the Year. Year after year spelled success. Bull Lea was the nation's leading sire five times and leading broodmare sire four times. He sired nine champions, fifty-eight stakes winners, and three Kentucky Derby winners. His progeny earned more than $13.5 million.

Through Bull Lea's brilliance, Calumet's star rose faster and shone more brightly than any other breeding establishment in history.

			Ajax
		Teddy	Rondeau
	Bull Dog		Spearmint
		Plucky Liege	Concertina
Bull Lea			Voter
1935 brown colt		Ballot	Cerito
	Rose Leaves		Trenton
		Colonial	Thankful Blossom

RACE RECORD	STARTS	1ST	2ND	3RD	EARNINGS
(Stakes in Parentheses)	27	10 (6)	7 (7)	3 (2)	$94,825

1937 LAFAYETTE STAKES

SILVER PITCHER & TRAY

The sterling silver pitcher was designed by William Gale and Son, New York, and made circa 1860. The silver-plated tray is also circa 1860. Both were presented for the first running of the Lafayette Stakes at Keeneland.

won by:
Chic Maud
at Keeneland Racecourse

1938 BLUE GRASS STAKES

SILVER-GILT CUP

A silver-gilt cup and cover with wood base made by Peter Guille Ltd. in New York, this was the trophy presented to the winning owner in lieu of the perpetual trophy. A Saratoga yearling purchase, Bull Lea was the first of Calumet's six Blue Grass Stakes winners. Oddly, the trophy is engraved with the wrong date. It should read April 28, 1938.

won by:
Bull Lea
at Keeneland Racecourse

THE LEXINGTON BOWL

This sterling silver fruit bowl is a replica of the perpetual trophy. Attributed to Lexington, Ky., silversmith George W. Stewart, circa 1854, the original bowl was presented by the citizens of the city to Dr. Elisha Warfield, owner of the great racehorse Lexington. Embossed on one side is a racing scene believed to depict the finish of a match race between Lexington and Le Comte in New Orleans in 1854. The inscription on the base reads as follows: Presented by the Citizens of Lexington, Ky. to Dr. Elisha Warfield as a Token of their Esteem for the Immortal Horse Lexington 1854.

won by **Bull Lea** *at Keeneland Racecourse*

SILVER-GILT URN

This silver-gilt footed urn with cover and wood base is a replica of the Joseph Widener Challenge Trophy donated by Joseph Widener. Made by Greenleaf and Crosky, the gold-washed sterling silver urn has the legend of the cup on its base and the past winners engraved around the middle of the trophy. Any owner who won the race twice retained the original trophy.

won by:
Bull Lea
at Hialeah Park

GOLD HORSESHOE

An additional trophy for the Widener, this gold-plated horseshoe made into an ashtray is one of the shoes Bull Lea wore during the running of the race.

won by:
Bull Lea
at Hialeah Park

The
1940s

Whirlaway

Never was a horse more primed for stardom than Whirlaway, the hand-some chestnut with the long, flowing tail who put Calumet on the horse-racing map. "Mr. Longtail" had plenty of personality quirks that endeared him to the public. And, of course, he could just plain outrun his opponents.

Foaled at Calumet Farm on April 2, 1938, Whirlaway was a son of British import Blenheim II and out of the Sweep mare Dustwhirl. At two Whirlaway proved to be a handful for trainer Ben Jones. The compact chestnut won his debut by a nose after exhibiting a trait he would become known for — bearing out in the stretch. He made fifteen more starts that season, winning six, including the Saratoga Special and the Hopeful, and earned $77,275, the most for a juvenile that year.

Jones devoted the winter to working on Whirlaway's bolting habit, even cutting out the blinker covering the colt's left eye to keep his attention on the inner rail. Willful and stubborn, the colt continued to run the way he wanted, arriving at the 1941 Kentucky Derby with victories in just a couple of allowances and a handicap. But something clicked in the Derby as Whirlaway swooped past his competition to win by eight lengths. He added easy wins in the Preakness and Belmont Stakes to become Calumet's first Triple Crown winner. He also won that year the Travers, American Derby, and Dwyer among his thirteen victories.

At four Whirlaway continued building his impressive career. He made twenty-two starts and won twelve, including the Jockey Club Gold Cup and the Brooklyn, Dixie, and Massachusetts handicaps. In forty-two starts at three and four he never finished worse than third.

Whirlaway was retired in 1943. He earned championship honors at two, three, and four and was named Horse of the Year in 1941 and '42. He stood at Calumet for seven years before being sold to French breeder Marcel Boussac in 1950. Whirlaway sired eighteen stakes winners. He died in France in 1953 at the age of fifteen.

			Swynford
Whirlaway 1938 chestnut colt	Blenheim II	Blandford	Blanche
		Malva	Charles O'Malley
			Wild Arum
	Dustwhirl	Sweep	Ben Brush
			Pink Domino
		Ormonda	Superman
			Princess Ormonde

RACE RECORD (Stakes in Parentheses)	STARTS	1ST	2ND	3RD	EARNINGS
	60	32 (22)	15 (13)	9 (5)	$561,161

GOLD MEDALLION

Made of 14-karat gold, the medallion represents one of two Futurity victories for Calumet Farm. In 1947 Citation won the 58th running. The reverse of the coin is engraved with the profile of a horse's head.

won by:
Some Chance
at Belmont Park

GOLD BOWL

Known as the Man o' War Cup, this gold-plated bowl was designed by Tiffany & Co. Whirlaway won the first of three Travers Stakes for Calumet, followed by Beau Prince (1961) and Alydar (1978).

won by:
Whirlaway
at Saratoga Racecourse

SILVER URN

This sterling silver urn with lid was made by J.E. & W. Barnard & S. Smith in London, circa 1868-1871. Standing more than two feet tall, the elaborate trophy was awarded for Whirlaway's last race of his second Horse of the Year season.

won by:
Whirlaway
at Fair Grounds Racecourse

SILVER URN

This trophy was made by Gorham Silver. Founded in 1831 in Providence, R.I., Gorham was often called upon to create trophies for major sporting events. In addition to trophies for horse racing, it created the trophies for the America's Cup for yachting, the Davis Cup for tennis, and the Borg-Warner trophy for the Indianapolis 500 for auto racing.

won by:
Whirlaway
at Narragansett Park

Mar-Kell

Claiborne Farm's A.B. Hancock put together a syndicate to purchase Blenheim II from the Aga Khan. Chief among the shareholders with a one-quarter interest was Warren Wright. This timely investment, like many others by Wright during the mid-thirties, would reap bountiful and seemingly everlasting rewards.

On February 21, 1939, Calumet's champion Nellie Flag foaled a bay filly by the English Derby winner. She was named Mar-Kell for Margaret Kelly, the wife of the mayor of Chicago and a friend of the Wrights.

A new trainer arrived in August 1939. Ben A. Jones and his son Jimmy would spearhead the Calumet runners through championship after championship for almost thirty years. Mar-Kell would be among the first.

A consistent performer, Mar-Kell showed flashes of brilliance.

A win in Saratoga's Spinaway Stakes proved her finest hour at two and moved her to the top of her age group. It's usually a long way from glory to goat, but for Mar-Kell it was a mere six furlongs. Actually, not even six furlongs, for in a fit of temper before the Matron Stakes, she acted up, was placed outside the stalls, and refused to leave the post. Thus ended Mar-Kell's hopes for a juvenile championship.

Mar-Kell would have to wait two years for her championship. A well-traveled girl, especially considering wartime restrictions, she raced at six different tracks during 1943, including a successful trip to Aqueduct.

As many have discovered, a trip to New York can make or break a championship bid. So, when a stellar field of fillies and mares approached the starting gate for the Beldame Handicap, the winner could claim pro tem leadership of the division.

No longer a flighty ingénue, the seasoned, consummate professional Mar-Kell atoned for her errant, youthful behavior.

Her decisive one-length triumph, along with her eight other wins (one of which was a victory over her Triple Crown-winning stablemate Whirlaway) and six seconds in eighteen starts, secured her the division title.

			Swynford
		Blandford	Blanche
	Blenheim II		Charles O'Malley
		Malva	Wild Arum
Mar-Kell			Man o' War
1939 bay filly		American Flag	Lady Comfey
	Nellie Flag		Luke McLuke
		Nellie Morse	La Venganza

* *Red in pedigree indicates Calumet-bred*

RACE RECORD	STARTS	1ST	2ND	3RD	EARNINGS
(Stakes in Parentheses)	53	17 (5)	17 (10)	3	$84,365

Twilight Tear

In 1944 Calumet Farm's Pensive won the Kentucky Derby and Preakness Stakes. He might have been the best colt in the barn, but he was not the best horse. That honor belonged to a filly, Twilight Tear.

While breeders spend a great deal of time and thought in preparing the perfect mating, Twilight Tear was the product of chance. When Bull Lea was injured and unexpectedly retired to the breeding shed, Warren Wright switched some of his lesser mares to his new stallion. One of those was the ill-tempered Lady Lark, whose main claim was that she descended from the family of the great Domino. The result of the pairing was a strapping bay filly whose performances would elevate the status of this unproven stallion prospect.

At two Twilight Tear was one of the best of her age and in some polls shared the championship with another daughter of Bull Lea, Durazna. A large, masculine filly, Twilight Tear won the Arlington Lassie Stakes in her second start, becoming Bull Lea's first stakes winner.

Twilight Tear's three-year-old campaign was long, arduous, and, without doubt, successful. She opened against older males and finished third. She would not be beaten again in eleven races. During this streak she ran short, she ran long, and she ran against the boys. After winning the Coaching Club American Oaks against the best fillies and defeating colts in the Skokie Handicap in track-record time, she defeated Pensive in the Arlington Classic.

Fillies from the Belair Stud double-teamed Twilight Tear in the Alabama Stakes at Saratoga. Thread o' Gold engaged the Calumet filly in a speed duel, allowing stablemate Vienna to post a three-quarters-length victory.

Twilight Tear solidified Horse of the Year honors with her Pimlico Special win. She annihilated Greentree Stable's Devil Diver by six lengths and equaled the track record. Devil Diver had been winning most of the major handicaps and was the leading older horse in the country. In addition to Horse of the Year honors, she was named champion three-year-old filly.

			Teddy
		Bull Dog	Plucky Liege
	Bull Lea		Ballot
		Rose Leaves	Colonial
Twilight Tear			Black Servant
1941 bay filly		Blue Larkspur	Blossom Time
	Lady Lark		Lucullite
		Ladana	Adana

RACE RECORD	STARTS	1ST	2ND	3RD	EARNINGS
(Stakes in Parentheses)	24	18 (10)	2 (2)	2	$202,165

SILVER TRAY

The sterling silver tray represents the first of Calume six victories in the CCA Oa Each filly to win the Oaks would be awarded a championship.

won by:
Twilight Tear
at Belmont Park

SILVER CUP

The silver cup was made by Schofield Company and presented by the Maryland Jockey Club. In 1952 the Pimlico Oaks became the Black-Eyed Susan. In addition to Twilight Tear, Calumet won with Wistful (1949), Real Delight (1952), Princess Turia (1956), and Davona Dale (1979).

won by:
Twilight Tear
at Pimlico Racecourse

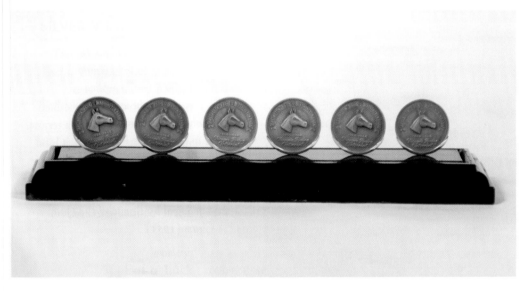

GOLD COINS

These gold coins were given by Arlington Park-Washington Park to honor the centennial anniversary (1844-1944). The coins on the base represent Twilight Tear's Skokie Handicap, in which she set a new track record; Twilight Tear's Princess Doreen Stakes; Sun Again's Equipoise Mile Handicap; Miss Keeneland's Cleopatra Stakes; Twilight Tear's Arlington Classic, in which she defeated her stablemate Pensive on her way to Horse of the Year honors; and Good Blood's Princess Pat Stakes.

won by:
Good Blood
Miss Keeneland
Sun Again
Twilight Tear (3)
at Arlington-Washington Park

Armed

Armed was a battle-hardened warrior who scraped his way to the top of the sport. He sprinted, stayed, carried weight, whatever was asked of him, but success on the track didn't come early or easily. He earned his place among horse racing's elite the hard way, by starting an exhausting eighty-one times in seven years. When Armed retired in 1950, he had won forty-one of those starts and placed in another thirty. His earnings of $817,475 made him the all-time leading money-earning gelding.

Armed was a member of Bull Lea's first foal crop, which included the brilliant fillies Twilight Tear and Durazna, and he was produced from the Chance Shot mare Armful, a former claimer. Gelded as a two-year-old because of his small size and studdish nature, Armed was used for a time as a lead pony for the yearlings at Calumet. At three Armed was sent to the track for serious training. He became a useful horse that year, winning three of seven starts, but his only forays into stakes company resulted in two dismal placings.

Armed also finished out of the money in his four-year-old debut; then he put it all together. After that race, Armed finished first or second twenty-two consecutive times. He earned his first championship in 1946 with victories that included the Widener, Suburban, and Washington Park handicaps and a special "Double Event," two races held a week apart at Tropical Park.

At six Armed reached his pinnacle, winning eleven of seventeen races. He captured the Widener and Washington Park handicaps again, plus the Stars and Stripes, McLennan, and Gulfstream Park handicaps. He was named champion handicap horse and Horse of the Year.

During his top years, Armed often carried and won under 130 pounds and finished second under 132 several times. He set eight track records from distances of a mile to a mile and a quarter. In the second part of the Double Event, he equaled his own track record for a mile and one-eighth.

Armed was retired in 1950 to Calumet, where he lived until his death in 1964.

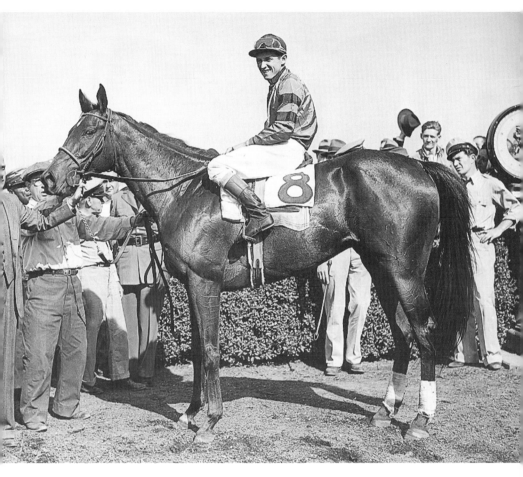

			Teddy
Armed 1941 brown gelding	Bull Lea	Bull Dog	
			Plucky Liege
		Rose Leaves	Ballot
			Colonial
	Armful	Chance Shot	Fair Play
			Quelle Chance
		Negrina	Luke McLuke
			Black Brocade

RACE RECORD

(Stakes in Parentheses)

	STARTS	1ST	2ND	3RD	EARNINGS
	81	41 (19)	20 (16)	10 (7)	$817,475

GOLD CUP

The two-handled 14-karat gold cup with cover and wood base was presented to Warren Wright for Armed's victory in the 1946 Widener Handicap. Calumet horses won the Widener eight times with five horses: Bull Lea (1939), Armed (1946, 1947), Coaltown (1949), Bardstown (1957, 1959), and Yorky (1961, 1962).

won by:
Armed
at Hialeah Park

SILVER URN

This George III sterling silver urn was made by R. & T. Green in London, circa 1708. The trophy was won by Armed, weighted with 130 pounds. Armed carried no fewer than 126 pounds at any time during the year and won with 130 six times. At year's end he was named champion older horse.

won by:
Armed
at Belmont Park

SILVER URN

The sterling silver urn with wood base was awarded to Calumet for its first Vineland Handicap. Good Blood, a daughter of Bull Lea—Diagnosis, won in 1946 and Bewitch in 1949.

won by:
Good Blood
at Garden State Park

SILVER URN

Made by Schofield and Company, this silver urn with cover has an acorn motif handle. Calumet had also won the Walden Stakes with Whirlaway in 1940. Fervent was a son of Blenheim II—Hug Again, one of Warren Wright's favorite mares.

won by:
Fervent
at Pimlico Racecourse

1947 FLAMINGO STAKES

GOLD CUP

The 14-karat gold trophy was made by Tiffany & Co. Engraved with a flamingo, it differs in design from the trophy of later decades. A son of Bull Lea—Unerring, Faultless was the first of four Flamingo winners for Calumet, followed by Citation (1948), Tim Tam (1958), and Alydar (1978).

won by:
Faultless
at Hialeah Park

1947 GULFSTREAM PARK HANDICAP

SILVER CUP

A sterling silver cup presented by Gulfstream Park, the trophy for the Gulfstream Park Handicap is 10 inches tall and 6 inches in diameter. This race was but one of the steps along the way to Armed's second champion older horse title and his Horse of the Year title.

won by:
Armed
at Gulfstream Park

SILVER WINE COOLER

This Old English Sheffield wine cooler, circa 1820, was presented to Calumet Farm for Armed's victory in the Stars and Stripes Handicap. His was the first of three consecutive victories for Calumet, followed by Citation (1948) and Coaltown (1949). Mark-Ye-Well added a fourth in 1955.

won by:
Armed
at Arlington Park

GOLD CUPS

The two 14-karat gold cups with cover and wood base were made by Shreve & Company in San Francisco to honor the owner and breeder. Calumet runners finished in the top three positions with the filly Bewitch beating stablemates Citation and Free America. The loss was the only one for Citation that year.

won by:
Bewitch
at Washington Park

Citation

At two and three Citation was two lengths shy of perfect. And in those two lengths lay a fallibility not his own. On each occasion had he been pressed to extend himself, he could have easily lengthened stride, found an extra measure of speed, and reeled in his opponent. But on each occasion, the jockey felt no need.

As a two-year-old, the sturdy son of Bull Lea and Hydroplane II won every race but the Washington Park Futurity. His stablemate Bewitch beat him by a length. Since Calumet owned the first three finishers in the race, there was no need to press Citation to overtake Bewitch. Citation finished the year undefeated and earned the two-year-old colt championship.

Early in his three-year-old season, Citation defeated all challengers, both his age and older, while wintering in Florida. At Havre de Grace in Maryland he started in the Chesapeake Trial Stakes. Carried wide on the muddy surface and with jockey Eddie Arcaro under orders not to use him up, Citation fell a length short of Saggy over the six furlongs.

Citation's victory in the subsequent Chesapeake Stakes began a string of sixteen. In five decades that record has been equaled but never broken. Included in that skein were a Triple Crown (the Kentucky Derby, Preakness, and Belmont), a Jockey Club Gold Cup, and a Pimlico Special. He was honored with the titles of champion three-year-old colt and Horse of the Year.

In the Tanforan Handicap, Citation sustained an injury, a painful osselet. Not responding well to treatment, Citation sat out the following year.

When he returned to racing, he was never quite the same. Although still very good, his performances were compromised by age, injury, and opponents that were younger and/or carried less weight.

The 1951 Hollywood Gold Cup win made Citation, by then worn and battle torn, the first horse to earn a million dollars. The old soldier was immediately retired to a stud career that produced moderate success.

			Teddy
		Bull Dog	
	Bull Lea		Plucky Liege
			Ballot
		Rose Leaves	
Citation			Colonial
1945 bay colt			Gainsborough
		Hyperion	
	Hydroplane II (GB)		Selene
			Hurry On
		Toboggan	
			Glacier

RACE RECORD

(Stakes in Parentheses)

STARTS	1ST	2ND	3RD	EARNINGS
45	32 (22)	10 (8)	2	$1,085,760

1948 ASHLAND STAKES

SILVER BOWL

The sterling silver punch bowl was crafted in the Georgian style by Peter Guille Ltd. in England. Calumet won the Ashland with Bewitch, Real Delight (1952), and Sugar and Spice (1980).

won by:
Bewitch
at Keeneland Racecourse

1948 JERSEY STAKES

SILVER-GILT COFFEE URN

A silver-gilt coffee urn with lid and wood base, the trophy is designed with snake handles and engraved with a feather and drape design on the body of the urn. Citation had already won the Kentucky Derby and the Preakness and contested the Jersey Stakes before his victory in the Belmont Stakes.

won by:
Citation
at Garden State Park

1948 GALLANT FOX HANDICAP

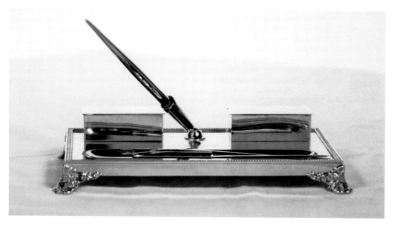

GOLD PEN AND PENCIL SET

The 14-karat gold pen and pencil set was designed by Cartier. It includes a gold pen and paper opener along with a desk tray.

won by: **Faultless** *at Jamaica Racetrack*

1948 JOCKEY CLUB GOLD CUP

GOLD CUP

A 10-karat gold cup and cover presented by the Westchester Racing Association, the cup was the third awarded to Calumet. Previous winners included Whirlaway (1942) and Pot o' Luck (1945). Ponder would add a fourth in 1949.

won by:
Citation
at Belmont Park

Wistful

Wistful was yet another of Calumet Farm's brilliant fillies of the 1940s. She followed on the heels of Twilight Tear, Bewitch, and Mar-Kell and was born the same year as stablemate Two Lea. But Wistful made sure she wasn't lost in the crowd when she became the first filly to win the old national Filly Triple Crown — the Kentucky Oaks, Pimlico Oaks, and Coaching Club American Oaks.

A homebred daughter of Sun Again out of the Blenheim II mare Easy Lass, Wistful came along a year after her half brother Coaltown (by Bull Lea), himself a contemporary of Citation. Coaltown was named Horse of the Year in 1949, the same year Wistful won the filly triple, resulting in their dam's being named Broodmare of the Year.

Wistful was lightly raced at two, breaking her maiden by six lengths in her second start. After a couple of tries at three, she got on a winning track at Hialeah, taking two allowance races. She then prepped for the Kentucky Oaks with a second in the Ashland at Keeneland and a win in allowance company at Churchill Downs. In the Oaks, she came from behind to win going away by four and a half lengths. In her next start, the Pimlico Oaks (now the Black-Eyed Susan), Wistful again moved up from well back to grab a three-quarters-length victory. Two weeks later at Belmont Park, she did it again, taking the CCA Oaks in the same come-from-behind manner. Her season of six wins in eleven starts, including the filly triple, earned Wistful champion three-year-old filly honors.

Wistful's early brilliance dimmed somewhat over the next three seasons, but she still claimed victories in several stakes, including the 1951 Whirlaway Stakes, Ben Ali, and Clark Handicap, all against males.

Wistful retired in 1952. Her best foal was the ill-fated Gen. Duke (by Bull Lea), who was the 1957 Kentucky Derby favorite before an injury knocked him out of the race. Winner of the Florida Derby, Gen. Duke became a wobbler and died a year later. Wistful herself died in 1964, one day before Bull Lea.

Wistful **1946 chestnut filly**	Sun Again	Sun Teddy	Teddy
			Sunmelia
		Hug Again	Stimulus
			Affection
	Easy Lass	Blenheim II	Blandford
			Malva
		Slow and Easy	Colin
			Shyness

Red in pedigree indicates Calumet-bred

RACE RECORD

(Stakes in Parentheses)

STARTS	1ST	2ND	3RD	EARNINGS
51	13 (8)	6 (5)	10 (6)	$213,060

Coaltown

Collapsed on the Arlington Park track in a pool of blood from a ruptured abscess in his throat, the unraced two-year-old Coaltown looked anything but a future champion.

Coaltown was sent back to the Kentucky farm and treated for a respiratory ailment that would plague him throughout his career. Changing his diet and painting his throat with iodine were part of the regimen. Coaltown was also trained to run differently. Trainers Ben and Jimmy Jones noticed that when he bowed his neck, the roar in his throat was more pronounced, so for morning works they engaged a steeplechase rider who rode with longer stirrups and a longer rein. This combination taught Coaltown to extend his neck and carry his head lower, thus relieving some of the stress on his breathing.

"Wheezy," as Coaltown was known around the barn, also wore a "throttle hood," a wool cloth tied around his neck to keep it warm and reduce constriction of his throat.

The treatment worked. Coaltown won his first four races as a three-year-old and set or equaled two track records. During the year he won five stakes, including the Blue Grass and Phoenix stakes at Keeneland and the Jerome Stakes at Belmont. He also finished second to stablemate and Triple Crown winner Citation in the Kentucky Derby. At year's end Coaltown was named champion sprinter.

With Citation sidelined in 1949, Coaltown starred. He blazed; he burned. Speed records fell like dominos. He equaled or set three world records and won twelve of fifteen races, finishing second in the others. He carried weight and ran long and short. Greentree Stable's Capot defeated Coaltown in the last two races of the year. As a result, the Horse of the Year title was split between the two. Coaltown, however, was top handicap horse in all polls.

Coaltown raced two more years, but never regained his earlier form. Retired to stud, he spent several years at Calumet before he was sold to Marcel Boussac in France, where he had an undistinguished career.

			Bull Dog	Teddy
Coaltown **1945 bay colt**	Bull Lea			Plucky Liege
		Rose Leaves	Ballot
			Colonial
	Easy Lass	Blenheim II	Blandford
			Malva
		Slow and Easy	Colin
			Shyness

• Red in pedigree indicates Calumet-bred

RACE RECORD (Stakes in Parentheses)	STARTS	1ST	2ND	3RD	EARNINGS
	39	23 (16)	6 (6)	3 (3)	$415,675

SILVER URN

Designed by Tiffany & Co., this sterling silver urn was awarded as the official trophy for the 1949 McLennan Handicap. Coaltown was the third Calumet representative to win the race. He followed Sun Again (1944) and Armed (1947). Calumet would add three more victories: Iron Liege (1958), On-and-On (1960), and Yorky (1961).

won by:
Coaltown
at Hialeah Park

1949 McLENNAN CHALLENGE CUP

SILVER URN

The sterling silver urn was made by Crichton Brothers and was the perpetual trophy for the McLennan Handicap. A stable that won the race three times would retain its possession. Coaltown's 1949 victory retired the trophy.

won by:
Coaltown
at Hialeah Park

THREE-SIDED SILVER VASE

Commissioned by the Thoroughbred Racing Associations, the trophy for the Triple Crown was designed by Cartier. Each side of the triangle is devoted to one of the Triple Crown events, the Kentucky Derby, the Preakness Stakes, and the Belmont Stakes, and contains the data for that race. Having not been commissioned until 1950, the first eight winners of the event were retroactive recipients. Calumet Farm received two trophies: Whirlaway (1941) and Citation (1948).

won by: **Citation** at Churchill Downs, Pimlico Racecourse, and Belmont Park

GOLD CUP

The famous Kentucky Derby trophy was commissioned by Col. Matt Winn for the 1924 Kentucky Derby. Designed by George Lewis Graff, it was crafted by Lemon & Sons of Louisville, Ky. Standing 22 inches tall without its marble base, the trophy has a 14-karat gold body. The horse and rider, handles, and other decorations are 18-karat gold. To commemorate the 75th running, the diamond jubilee trophy (1949) has a diamond-studded horseshoe on the body. Inset is Citation's Kentucky Derby trophy (1948), an example of the traditional prize. Calumet has won the Kentucky Derby more than any other owner, eight times. In addition to Ponder's diamond jubilee victory, Calumet won with Whirlaway (1941), Pensive (1944), Citation (1948), Hill Gail (1952), Iron Liege (1957), Tim Tam (1958), and Forward Pass (1968).

won by: **Ponder** *at Churchill Downs*

SILVER REPLICA OF WOODLAWN VASE

The Woodlawn Vase has been called the most valuable trophy in sport. It was created by Tiffany & Co. in 1860 as a trophy for the Woodlawn Racing Association of Louisville, Ky. This sterling silver replica was made by Kirk Stieff of Baltimore, Md., and awarded to the winning owner. Calumet has won the Preakness a record seven times: Whirlaway (1941), Pensive (1944), Faultless (1947), Citation (1948), Fabius (1956), Tim Tam (1958), and Forward Pass (1968).

won by: **Citation** *at Pimlico Racecourse*

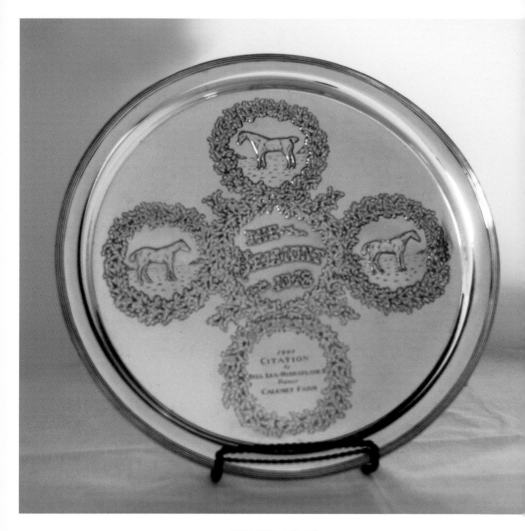

SILVER TRAY

Made by Peter Guille Ltd., this silver trophy is awarded to the winning owner of the Belmont Stakes. The three horses engraved on the tray represent Eclipse, Herod, and Matchem, foundation sires for all of today's Thoroughbreds. The names of all the winners of the Belmont are engraved on the back of the tray.

won by: **Citation** at Belmont Park

The
1950s

Bewitch

Bewitch seemed to cast a spell over her opponents, mesmerizing them with speed. The sweet-tempered, dainty filly was at her best going between five and seven furlongs, but as she matured she stretched her speed effectively to nine furlongs.

Foaled in 1945, Bewitch was by Calumet stalwart Bull Lea out of the Wildair mare Potheen, whom Calumet owner Warren Wright had purchased as a three-year-old for five hundred dollars. Potheen produced 1945 Jockey Club Gold Cup winner Pot o' Luck and stakes winner Theen for Wright, and she was named Broodmare of the Year in 1947.

Bewitch had a great deal to do with her dam's receiving this honor. As a two-year-old in 1947, Bewitch was virtually unstoppable, running ten times and losing once. In her debut at Keeneland, she zipped four furlongs in :46 1/5 to win by six lengths, then repeated that performance a week later in :46 flat. Trained by Ben and Jimmy Jones, Bewitch went on that year to capture seven stakes, including the Debutante, Arlington Lassie, and Washington Futurity.

She rose to prominence in the Washington Futurity by beating stablemates Citation and Free America, who finished second and third, respectively. For her efforts Bewitch was named champion two-year-old filly.

At three Bewitch won four of six starts, including the Ashland and Modesty stakes. She had an up-and-down season at four, running thirteen times and winning four, including the Inaugural Handicap in track-record time at Churchill. She also went beyond a mile for the first time that year, taking the mile and one-sixteenth Vineland Handicap. She ended the season as champion handicap mare.

Bewitch raced two more years, but only managed to win four times in twenty-six starts before being retired. She ended her career with earnings of $462,605, making her the leading money-earning filly at the time. As a broodmare, she could not continue her dam's success. She had only two foals, both of which died before reaching the racetrack. Bewitch died in 1962.

			Teddy
		Bull Dog	Plucky Liege
	Bull Lea		Ballot
		Rose Leaves	Colonial
Bewitch			Broomstick
1945 brown filly		Wildair	Verdure
	Potheen		Hamburg
		Rosie O'Grady	Cherokee Rose II

RACE RECORD
(Stakes in Parentheses)

STARTS	1ST	2ND	3RD	EARNINGS
55	20 (15)	10 (7)	11 (4)	$462,605

1950 BLACK HELEN HANDICAP

SILVER PITCHER

This sterling silver pitcher measures 9 1/4 inches tall. Bewitch won the Black Helen by seven lengths for her only stakes win of 1950. Calumet also won the Black Helen with Amoret (1957), Rosewood (1959), and Princess Arle (1964).

won by:
Bewitch
at Hialeah Park

1951 VANITY HANDICAP

SILVER PLATTER

This oval sterling silver platter was created by the San Francisco-based silversmiths, Shreve & Company. The Vanity was Bewitch's sole stakes win of 1951.

won by: **Bewitch** *at Hollywood Park*

1951 HOLLYWOOD GOLD CUP

GOLD CENTERPIECE

This 14-karat gold oval centerpiece with a flower mesh top was designed by Tiffany & Co. The trophy rests on a gold-edged mirror (not pictured). Citation broke the $1 million mark in earnings in this race to become horse racing's first equine millionaire.

won by: **Citation** at Hollywood Park

1952 DEBUTANTE STAKES

SILVER PITCHER

This English silver-plated pitcher was imported by Wakefield-Scearce, the Kentucky-based antiques dealer and silversmith. The pitcher has a leaf design etched into its body and ornate scrollwork on the handle and around the foot. That same meet Calumet's Hill Gail won the Kentucky Derby and Real Delight won the Kentucky Oaks.

won by:
Bubbley
at Churchill Downs

65

Two Lea

Two Lea may not have been the most brilliant of Calumet Farm's runners, but she was one of its toughest. That toughness carried the bay filly through four seasons of racing, during which foot ailments frequently plagued her.

As a yearling, well before she started racing, Two Lea had to contend with foot problems, including an infection and ringbone. The daughter of Bull Lea and Two Bob got to the races in August of her two-year-old year, 1948, and ran three times, winning in her final start. At three Two Lea was nearly perfect, winning six of seven starts and finishing second in the lone loss. Her stablemate Wistful also was three that year, but trainers Ben and Jimmy Jones kept the fillies mostly separated. Wistful captured the Oaks triple while Two Lea quietly went about winning the Princess Doreen, Cleopatra (over Wistful), and Artful stakes. She was named co-champion three-year-old filly with Wistful.

At four, Two Lea added a victory in the Santa Margarita Handicap, and then took on males. She finished second to stablemate Ponder in the Santa Anita Maturity, then third to Noor and stablemate Citation in the Santa Anita Handicap. She was named champion older mare.

In late summer of 1950, her foot problems resurfaced. She was sidelined through 1951. Trainer Jimmy Jones decided to bring her back in May of 1952. She ran four times that month, winning an allowance and finishing second in the Milady Handicap (to younger stablemate A Gleam) along the way. She then captured the Vanity Handicap over Wistful. That July she took the Ramona Handicap in a dead heat, then won the Hollywood Gold Cup over males. She added two more stakes victories that year before finally being retired.

Sent to Calumet, Two Lea was just as good as a broodmare. She produced Kentucky Derby and Preakness winner Tim Tam (by Tom Fool) and multiple stakes winners On-and-On and Pied d'Or (both by Nasrullah). Two Lea died in 1973.

			Teddy
		Bull Dog	Plucky Liege
	Bull Lea		Ballot
		Rose Leaves	Colonial
Two Lea 1946 bay filly			Sweep
		The Porter	Ballet Girl
	Two Bob		Chicle
		Blessings	Mission Bells

RACE RECORD (Stakes in Parentheses)	STARTS	1ST	2ND	3RD	EARNINGS
	26	15 (9)	6 (4)	3 (1)	$309,250

1953 MILADY HANDICAP

SILVER BOWL

This silver bowl was awarded to A Gleam for her second win in the Milady. She had won the previous year's running as well, receiving a silver platter for that victory.

won by:
A Gleam
at Hollywood Park

1954 GOLDEN GATE FUTURITY

CRYSTAL DECANTERS

This trophy includes two square spirit decanters from Stuart Crystal in England, set in an engraved silver holder created by Shreve & Company. Trentonian won the inaugural running of the event for Calumet.

won by:
Trentonian
at Golden Gate Fields

1956 BUCKEYE HANDICAP

SILVER URN

In tribute to the race name, a buck's antlers serve as handles on each side. They surround a footed urn with a scalloped rim. The Buckeye was run at the now-defunct Randall Park in Ohio.

won by:
Bardstown
at Randall Park

1956 ACORN STAKES

SILVER TUREEN

Two Calumet homebred fillies, Beyond and Princess Turia, deadheated to win this Sheffield-plated silver soup tureen or chafing dish.

won by:
Beyond and Princess Turia in a dead heat
at Belmont Park

SILVER URN

Standing 26 inches tall, this impressive antique English silver urn is the largest trophy in the collection. Made in London in 1838 by silversmith J.E. Terry, it is an adaptation of the Warwick vase. Made of stone, the original was found in 1770 among the ruins of a villa in Tivoli, Italy, built by Roman Emperor Hadrian. Taken to England, it was purchased by the Earl of Warwick. This urn was obtained as a challenge cup by C.V. Whitney in honor of his horse, Equipoise, for whom the race was named. The trophy was engraved by Cartier to read: "In memory of Equipoise whose world's record mile run in 1:34 2/5 crowned his famous racing career." One of Equipoise's shoes, silver-plated, rests inside the cover. The challenge cup went to any owner who won the race three times. Calumet won with Sun Again (1944), Fervent (1948), and Bardstown.

won by: **Bardstown** *at Arlington Park*

1956 DERBY TRIAL

SILVER TUREEN

This silver-plated soup tureen with cover dates to circa 1855. The piece was created by Elkington & Co., Birmingham, England. Company founder G.R. Elkington perfected and patented electroplating of silver in 1840.

won by: **Fabius**
at Churchill Downs

1957 FLORIDA DERBY

SILVER-GILT BOWL

This silver-gilt punch powl with cover rests on a walnut wood base. A horse's head finial decorates the cover, while horse's heads in stalls connect the bowl to the base. Gen. Duke was the first of five Florida Derby winners for Calumet.

won by:
Gen. Duke
at Gulfstream Park

GOLD BOWL

This simple 14-karat gold bowl features Calumet's silks hand-enameled on the front. The cup, made by Caldwell & Co. in Philadelphia, originally sat on a wood base. The back (inset) is etched with a pastoral mare and foal scene.

won by: **Princess Turia**
at Delaware Park

1957 JERSEY STAKES

SILVER-GILT COFFEE URN

This silver-gilt coffee urn with wood base is similar in design to the one awarded Citation in 1948 for his Jersey Stakes win. Calumet also won the Jersey in 1956 with Fabius, who also received the same type of trophy.

won by:
Iron Liege
at Garden State Park

SILVER PLATE

This silver plate went to A Glitter for giving Calumet its fourth victory in the race. Her win gave the farm permanent possession of the race's challenge cup.

won by:
A Glitter
at Belmont Park

1958 MONMOUTH OAKS

SILVER CUP

This silver three-handled and -footed "loving cup" was designed by Tiffany & Co. A Glitter's Oaks win was Calumet's first at Monmouth Park.

won by:
A Glitter
at Monmouth Park

A Glitter

If there were such a thing as an equine diva, it was A Glitter. Her ability was a blessing; her quirks, a curse.

A daughter of Khaled out of the good racemare A Gleam, this aptly named filly came to hand late in her two-year-old season. Large and well made, A Glitter won three races within eleven days and entered the Selima Stakes as the favorite. She brought with her the bad habits of drifting out in the stretch and tail switching. In the Selima trial she drifted so wide that Bill Hartack, her jockey, thought there was a physical problem. She held on to win that race but was not so fortunate in the stakes. As she gained the lead, she bolted to the outside, dropped back, and finished third.

Her errant behavior continued in the early part of her three-year-old season, although she never exhibited bad habits in morning works. Sorely trying the patience of her trainer, Jimmy Jones, who called her "a mean, switch-tailed thing," she was almost vanned to the farm as a better brood-mare prospect than runner. However, one of Calumet's grooms needed another horse to rub, so she was sent instead to Calumet's stable in the East, a fortunate thing for Calumet.

A Glitter became a changed girl. Patience, a different groom with a gentle touch, and a change in training methods worked wonders. She seemed to think running and winning might not be such a bad idea. Although she continued to switch her tail, she didn't bear out so badly, and her temperamental behavior seemed on the wane. She started winning, first in the Betsy Ross Stakes. Three victories later she took the Coaching Club American Oaks, Calumet's fourth, and retired the permanent trophy. She later added the Monmouth Oaks and finished second in the Beldame and third in the Vineland. Not recognized in the main polls, A Glitter won her championship based on a mathematical scoring system.

A Glitter continued to race at four and added the Modesty Handicap to her collection. She retired to Calumet as a broodmare but did not live up to her genetic potential.

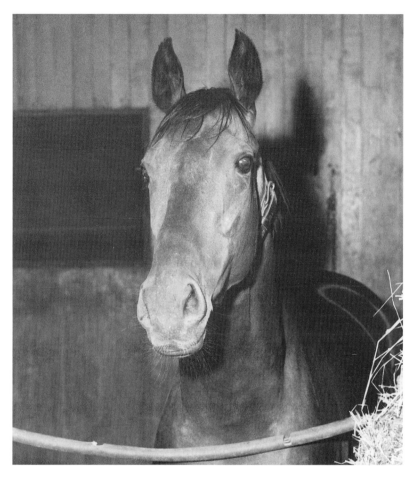

A Glitter 1955 brown filly	Khaled	Hyperion	Gainsborough
			Selene
		Eclair	Ethnarch
			Black Ray
	A Gleam	Blenheim II	Blandford
			Malva
		Twilight Tear	Bull Lea
			Lady Lark

• Red in pedigree indicates Calumet-bred

RACE RECORD

(Stakes in Parentheses)	STARTS	1ST	2ND	3RD	EARNINGS
	39	13 (4)	3 (2)	7 (5)	$196,370

SILVER-GILT CUP

Dating to Revolutionary times, this silver-gilt two-handled cup with cover is known as the Singleton Cup. The permanent trophy for the Coaching Club American Oaks, it goes to any stable whose horses win three runnings of the race. Calumet Farm became the third stable to retire the trophy, following Walter M. Jeffords and King Ranch. Jeffords retired the cup with winners Florence Nightingale, Edith Cavell, and Bateau in the 1920s, and King Ranch won with Dawn Play, Too Timely, and Scattered.

Calumet Farm won the CCA Oaks with Twilight Tear (1944), Wistful (1949), Real Delight (1952), and A Glitter, the last three earning the challenge cup. Calumet later won the race with Our Mims (1977) and Davona Dale (1979).

won by: **A Glitter** *at Belmont Park*

SILVER CUP

This trophy is an English silver two-handled cup with cover. Iron Liege's victory in the McLennan was the fourth in the race for Calumet.

won by:
Iron Liege
at Hialeah Park

SILVER COCKTAIL SHAKER AND CUPS

An unusual but useful choice for a trophy, this silver cocktail set, made by Fisher Co., contains a plain tray, six cups, and a 10-inch tall cocktail shaker. Calumet also won the Fountain of Youth with Gen. Duke (1957) and Beau Prince (1961).

won by:
Tim Tam
at Gulfstream Park

1958 FLORIDA DERBY

GOLD BOWL

This gold bowl is engraved with t state of Florida and its seal on the front. Other scenes from Florida history engraved on the bowl incl pirates and citrus fruit. The bowl sits on a mirrored base.

won by:
Tim Tam
at Gulfstream Park

1958 DERBY TRIAL

SILVER COFFEE URN

This English silver-plated coffee urn with lid, circa 1860, was imported by Krull of Louisville, Ky. Tim Tam is the last horse to win both the Derby Trial and the Kentucky Derby.

won by:
Tim Tam
at Churchill Downs

The
1960s

1960 ORANGE BOWL HANDICAP

SILVER BOWL

This silver-plated punch bowl was made by F.B. Roger Silver Co. It has a plain foot and the bowl's rim is decorated with grapes, shells, and flowers. Calumet had previously won this stakes with Bardstown (1959).

won by:
On-and-On
at Tropical Park

1960 BROOKLYN HANDICAP

SILVER CUP

This trophy is an English silver cup and cover from the George III era by Benjamin Brewood of London, England, circa 1766. The victory of Calumet's son of Nasrullah—Two Lea is the farm's only win in this event.

won by:
On-and-On
at Aqueduct Racetrack

1961 FOUNTAIN OF YOUTH STAKES

SILVER URN

This silver-plated urn is shown without its pedestal and wood base. Beau Prince added this trophy to the Calumet collection, giving the farm its third win in this important Kentucky Derby prep.

won by:
Beau Prince
at Gulfstream Park

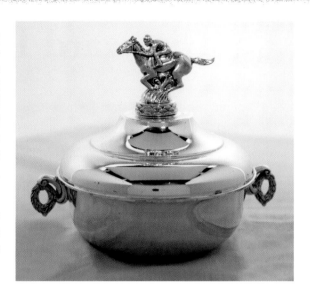

1962 MICHIGAN MILE

SILVER TROPHY

An unusual addition, this trophy is designed to resemble the state of Michigan. Attached is a photograph of the runners at the wire.

won by:
Beau Prince
at Detroit Racecourse

Forward Pass

During the 1960s Calumet Farm suffered a reversal of fortune. Its premier stallion was old and pensioned. The endless stream of stakes winners from the forties and fifties was a trickle. The farm whose horses had won seven Kentucky Derbys had not had an entry since 1958. Forward Pass would change all that. But not without a footnote.

Two great Calumet families had joined to create the large but well-proportioned homebred. His sire was On-and-On, a son of Two Lea and Calumet's main Derby prospect at one time. Forward Pass' dam, Princess Turia, contended for a championship herself.

Forward Pass drew attention when he won the Flash Stakes at Saratoga at two. Following the traditional Calumet path for Derby hopefuls, he wintered in Florida. He won the Hibiscus and Everglades stakes at Hialeah, and became a serious contender with his Florida Derby victory. Trainer Henry Forrest shipped Forward Pass to Keeneland for the Blue Grass Stakes, where the colt turned in one of his best performances, obliterating the field by five lengths in near track-record time.

The Kentucky Derby was next. Calumet had won the Derby with Citation ('48) and Tim Tam ('58). Would destiny continue the tradition?

Forward Pass did win the 1968 Derby, but not by crossing the finish line first. He became a footnote in history as the only winner by disqualification. Urine samples taken from Dancer's Image contained the illegal substance phenylbutazone, causing the racing stewards to take down his number and declare Forward Pass the official winner.

Forward Pass won a seventh Preakness for Calumet, romping by six lengths. Had he won the Belmont, racing would have had its first Triple Crown winner by default. That was not to be. He finished second to Greentree Stable's Stage Door Johnny.

Forward Pass did go on to win the American Derby and finish second in the Travers. Named champion three-year-old colt, he retired to stud at Calumet before being sold to Japan.

			Nearco
		Nasrullah	Mumtaz Begum
	On-and-On		Bull Lea
		Two Lea	Two Bob
Forward Pass			Hyperion
1965 bay colt		Heliopolis	Drift
	Princess Turia		Blue Larkspur
		Blue Delight	Chicleight

• Red in pedigree indicates Calumet-bred

RACE RECORD

(Stakes in Parentheses)

STARTS	1ST	2ND	3RD	EARNINGS
23	10 (8)	4 (2)	2 (1)	$580,631

SILVER MEMENTO

In 1963 silver orbs resting on black wooden bases were presented to commemorate induction to Racing's Hall of Fame in Saratoga Springs, N.Y. Elected that year were two Calumet champions from the forties, both Horse of the Year title holders: Twilight Tear and Armed.

earned by:
Twilight Tear
Armed

1968 AMERICAN DERBY

GOLD CUP

This gold cup with a wood base was made by Shreve & Company. Forward Pass' victory in the 1968 running gave Calumet an unprecedented seven victories in the Chicago fixture. Calumet had won the race with Whirlaway (1941), Fervent (1947), Citation (1948), Ponder (1949), Mark-Ye-Well (1952), and Beau Prince (1961).

won by:
Forward Pass
at Arlington Park

The
1970s

1977 FANTASY STAKES

GOLD CUP

This gold-plated sterling cup with cover was made by Mark Scearce of Shelbyville, Ky. It stands 17 inches tall from the base to the horse and jockey finial. The victory in this event marked the start of a brief resurgence in Calumet's racing luck. It was also the first stakes victory in a championship season for Our Mims. Calumet would win this race with another champion, Davona Dale, in 1979.

won by:
Our Mims
at Oaklawn Park

1977 ALABAMA STAKES

SILVER TRAY

This trophy is a large, rectangular, two-handled tea tray. It is English silver in a George III style. Our Mims' victory was Calumet's first Alabama Stakes win.

won by: **Our Mims** *at Saratoga Racecourse*

BRONZE STATUETTE

This bronze statuette is Calumet Farm's first Eclipse Award. The Eclipse Award, a 4-inch bronze of Eclipse mounted on a rosewood base, was created by Adalin Wichman. Started in 1971, the awards to honor the outstanding racehorses of each division were named for Eclipse, the great racehorse and sire of the 18th century.

won by:
Our Mims

SILVER COFFEE URN

This silver coffee urn is Old English Sheffield, circa 1785. Standing on four ball feet, the trophy is 15 inches tall. Alydar's victory was the colt's first stakes win and his first win over his archrival Affirmed.

won by:
Alydar
at Belmont Park

Alydar

A lydar became one of horse racing's most beloved and well-respected campaigners more for his close losses to archrival Affirmed than his wins. Alydar was part of Calumet Farm's brief return to glory in the late 1970s. His half sister Our Mims and the dual Filly Triple Crown winner Davona Dale also were part of the resurgence. The two fillies became champions, an honor that eluded Alydar. Not that it really mattered.

A handsome chestnut son by Raise a Native out of the On-and-On mare Sweet Tooth, Alydar hit the racetrack in the summer of 1978 and ran right into Affirmed. As two-year-olds, Alydar and Affirmed met six times, Affirmed getting the upper hand four times. Alydar bested his rival in the Great American and Champagne stakes at Belmont Park. But Affirmed got the championship.

At three the two colts took different routes to the Triple Crown. Alydar stayed on the East Coast and Affirmed went west. Alydar came up to the Kentucky Derby having won all four of his starts that spring, including the Blue Grass Stakes. But in the Derby, Affirmed, who also was undefeated that season, claimed victory over a late-closing Alydar. In the Preakness, the two colts finished just a neck apart, with Affirmed again the winner. The Belmont was the climactic event between the two gallant colts. They battled down the stretch, neither giving an inch, until Affirmed thrust his head in front at the wire. Alydar had lost the Triple Crown but earned the admiration of racing fans everywhere. Later that season, he faced Affirmed one last time, in the Travers at Saratoga. Affirmed won, but was disqualified for interfering with Alydar, who had come on to finish second.

Injury then sidelined Alydar, who returned at four but not at the same level. He was retired in July of 1979. At stud he was a sensation, siring seventy-seven stakes winners, including Horses of the Year Alysheba and Criminal Type and champions Easy Goer, Turkoman, and Althea. Alydar died in 1990, and soon after Calumet fell into bankruptcy and was sold at public auction in 1992 to Henryk de Kwiatkowski.

		Native Dancer	Polynesian
	Raise a Native		Geisha
		Raise You	Case Ace
			Lady Glory
Alydar 1975 chestnut colt		On-and-On	Nasrullah
	Sweet Tooth		Two Lea
		Plum Cake	Ponder
			Real Delight

Red in pedigree indicates Calumet-bred

RACE RECORD
(Stakes in Parentheses)

STARTS	1ST	2ND	3RD	EARNINGS
26	14 (11)	9 (9)	1 (1)	$957,195

1977 SAPLING STAKES

SILVER CONE

The trophy for the Sapling Stakes is of cone-shaped silver and stands on a green marble base. The handles are whip ends, and a stirrup holds the cone. A free-standing gold sapling stands in front of the cone. Alydar's win marked Calumet's first in this stakes. The very next year Calumet's Tim the Tiger won the Sapling Stakes as well.

won by:
Alydar
at Monmouth Park

1978 BLUE GRASS STAKES

GOLD JULEP CUP

This 14-karat gold julep cup has become the traditional trophy for a stakes win at Keeneland. It was made by Wakefield-Scearce of Shelbyville, Ky. Calumet had won this key Derby prep with Bull Lea (1938), Ocean Wave (1943), Faultless (1947), Coaltown (1948), and Forward Pass (1968).

won by: **Alydar** at Keeneland Racecourse

SILVER CONE

The newer version of the Flamingo Stakes trophy is a silver cone with gilt flamingos surrounding the base. The cone stands on a six-sided piece of pink, white, and gray marble. Alydar's victory marked the beginning of his trail to the Triple Crown, where he became the first horse to finish second in all three races.

won by:
Alydar
at Hialeah Park

SILVER CONE

This silver cone with gilt orchid is the new version of the trophy for the Florida Derby. Alydar followed his Flamingo Stakes win with this traditional Florida prep race for the Kentucky Derby. Calumet runners won the Florida Derby five times: Gen. Duke (1957), Tim Tam (1958), Forward Pass (1968), Eastern Fleet (1971), and Alydar.

won by:
Alydar
at Gulfstream Park

SILVER TUREEN

The silver soup tureen with cover is Old English Sheffield, circa 1825. The victory by the son of Nashua— Rose Court was Calumet's first in the Cowdin Stakes and an important step in reviving Calumet's heritage.

won by:
Tim the Tiger
at Belmont Park

SILVER CUP

The silver cup with cover is English Sheffield, circa 1906. Alydar's decisive 10-length victory over older horses in this Saratoga fixture set him up for a meeting with Affirmed in the Travers Stakes, the rivals' final meeting. This was Calumet's first victory in the Whitney.

won by:
Alydar
at Saratoga Racecourse

SILVER JULEP CUPS

This is one of 12 julep cups in a mahogany case, the now traditional trophy for the Kentucky Oaks. A horseshoe is affixed to each julep cup. Davona Dale became Calumet's sixth winner of the Oaks, the first leg of the old Filly Triple Crown.

won by:
Davona Dale
at Churchill Downs

SILVER BOWL

This sterling silver bowl awarded to the winner has black-eyed susans on the handles. Its wood base is not shown. Davona Dale was the fifth Calumet filly to win this event, the second leg of the old Filly Triple Crown.

won by:
Davona Dale
at Pimlico Racecourse

Davona Dale

Davona Dale was truly the last great star for Calumet Farm. She came on the scene two years after Our Mims' championship season and one year after Alydar's great rivalry with Affirmed. She wasted little time making a name for herself.

Davona Dale was a complete Calumet-bred, from her stakes-winning sire Best Turn, to her dam, Royal Entrance, a daughter of Calumet's 1958 Kentucky Derby winner Tim Tam. Davona Dale had a brief juvenile campaign, winning both her starts, including the Holly Stakes.

At three she started thirteen times, winning eight races and placing in two. After losing her first two starts, Davona Dale went on an eight-race win streak. She won the Bonnie Miss Stakes at Gulfstream Park and then romped in the Debutante at Fair Grounds. From there, she traveled to Oaklawn Park to win the Fantasy Stakes before heading to Churchill Downs.

In the Kentucky Oaks Davona Dale began a truly historic trek. She won that race easily and two weeks later added the Black-Eyed Susan at Pimlico. Trainer John Veitch sent her to New York to attempt the Filly Triple Crown. She won the first leg, the Acorn, and devastated the field for the second leg, the Mother Goose, by ten lengths. She won the final leg, the Coaching Club American Oaks, by a mere eight lengths. With the CCA Oaks win, Davona Dale accomplished something no filly before or since has done — she captured two filly triples, the old National Filly Triple Crown of the Kentucky Oaks, Black-Eyed Susan (formerly Pimlico Oaks), and CCA Oaks, and, the New York Triple, now the Triple Tiara.

Davona Dale earned champion three-year-old filly honors and retired after an abbreviated four-year-old season with eleven wins in eighteen starts and earnings of $641,612. At the November 1991 dispersal of Calumet stock at Keeneland, Davona Dale was purchased by John Magnier of Coolmore Stud for $220,000. She produced several foals in Ireland before dying in 1997 while foaling.

			Royal Charger
Davona Dale **1976 bay filly**	Best Turn	Turn-to	Source Sucree
		Sweet Clementine	Swaps
			Miz Clementine
	Royal Entrance	Tim Tam	Tom Fool
			Two Lea
		Prince's Gate	Sun Again
			Siena Way

• Red in pedigree indicates Calumet-bred

RACE RECORD
(Stakes in Parentheses)

STARTS	1ST	2ND	3RD	EARNINGS
18	11 (10)	2 (2)	1	$641,612

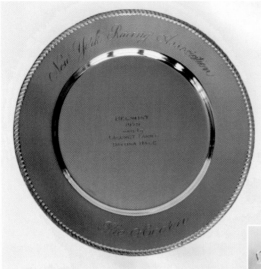

SILVER-GILT PLATE

This silver-gilt plate, made by James Robison, is the trophy for the first leg of the New York Filly Triple Crown. Inset is the trophy for the Mother Goose Stakes, an antique English silver tray with inkwells made in Sheffield by T. Bradbury & Sons in 1906.

won by:
Davona Dale *at Belmont Park*

SILVER TRAY

This large silver tray is English in the style of George III and was made in London, circa 1908. The CCA Oaks is the third leg of the old Filly Triple Crown and the New York Filly Triple Crown.

won by: **Davona Dale** *at Belmont Park*

SILVER-GILT URN

This George III style silver-gilt urn with cover and wood base is decorated with a shell and leaf design. It was created by Robert Garrard in London, circa 1816. The cup was presented to Calumet for Davona Dale's winning of the New York Filly Triple Crown. She was the first filly to win both the New York series and the old filly triple crown series.

won by:
Davona Dale

SILVER PUNCH BOWL

The silver-plated punch bowl and ladle were presented to Calumet for Before Dawn's victory. Before Dawn was the last champion for the Calumet Farm of old.

won by: **Before Dawn** *at Fair Grounds Racecourse*

Before Dawn

Before Dawn would be the final heirloom in the five-decade legacy of the old guard Calumet Farm.

Trained by John Veitch, Before Dawn showed promise from the outset, winning her first race by more than six lengths. Her victory in the Fashion Stakes by more than five lengths established her as the leading two-year-old filly of the summer, if not the leading two-year-old in general.

More stakes wins followed, despite some shin trouble typical for two-year-olds. At Saratoga, Before Dawn annihilated the field assembled for the Spinaway Stakes by more than seven lengths. She wheeled back eleven days later to win the Astarita Stakes at Belmont by two and a half lengths, a narrow margin by her standards.

In her final start of the year against fillies, she once again proved her superiority. The Matron Stakes was little more than a showcase for Before Dawn's superior talent; she won by six and a half lengths.

Before Dawn had faced the best of the fillies, defeating them by an average of five and three-quarters lengths. Only one challenge remained: the colts. Veitch used the Champagne Stakes at Belmont to test her mettle. She did not win, but she did not disappoint. Only one beat her, Timely Writer.

Before Dawn won her first three races in Florida before shipping to Louisiana for the Fair Grounds Oaks. She overcame a poor start and steadly improved her position, posting a two-length victory. Her third-place finish in Oaklawn Park's Fantasy Stakes marked her first loss against fillies.

Keeping a long-standing tradition, Before Dawn attempted to become the seventh Calumet filly to win the Kentucky Oaks. She almost succeeded. The mile and an eighth distance probably lay on the periphery of her ability, but she held on gamely to finish second to Blush With Pride.

After two poor performances she retired to Calumet.

The legend of Calumet Farm is circular and complete. The story ended as it began: champion two-year-old fillies separated by a circumference of nearly fifty years.

			Raise a Native	Native Dancer
				Raise You
	Raise a Cup		Spring Sunshine	Nashua
Before Dawn				Real Delight
1979 bay filly			Tim Tam	Tom Fool
	Moonbeam			Two Lea
			A Gleam	Blenheim II
				Twilight Tear

• Red in pedigree indicates Calumet-bred

RACE RECORD
(Stakes in Parentheses)

STARTS	1ST	2ND	3RD	EARNINGS
14	9 (7)	2 (2)	1 (1)	$432,855

Honor Roll

Hall of Fame *(year inducted)*

Ben Jones (1958)

Jimmy Jones (1959)

Alydar (1989)

Armed (1963)

Bewitch (1977)

Citation (1959)

Coaltown (1983)

Davona Dale (1985)

Real Delight (1987)

Tim Tam (1985)

Twilight Tear (1963)

Two Lea (1982)

Whirlaway (1959)

Champions *(year elected)*

A Glitter (1958)

Armed (1946-47)

Barbizon (1956)

Before Dawn (1981)

Bewitch (1947, 1949)

Citation (1947-48, 1951)

Coaltown (1949)

Davona Dale (1979)

Forward Pass (1968)

Mar-Kell (1943)

Nellie Flag (1934)

Our Mims (1977)

Real Delight (1952)

Tim Tam (1958)

Twilight Tear (1944)

Two Lea (1949-50)

Whirlaway (1940-42)

Wistful (1949)

Ben (left) and Jimmy Jones hold three of Calumet's biggest stars of the 1940s: Bewitch (left), Armed (middle), and Citation (right).

Acknowledgments

The editors would like to acknowledge the following people for their invaluable assistance and oftentimes hard work in compiling this book.

Margaret B. Glass
Calumet Farm secretary, 1940 to 1982

At the Kentucky Horse Park:
Bill Cooke, director of the International Museum of the Horse
Jenifer Raisor, curator of collections

At the Keeneland Library:
Cathy Schenck and Phyllis Rogers

The Blood-Horse chief photographer Anne M. Eberhardt

Photographer Barbara D. Livingston

Photo Credits

Trophy photos by Anne M. Eberhardt

Trophies on pps. 65 (Hollywood Gold Cup); 103, 106, 107 (New York Filly Triple Crown) by Barbara D. Livingston

Cover trophy photos by Lee Thomas; Cover photo of Citation (The Blood-Horse); Back cover of Citation (Churchill Downs)

Photo of Margaret Glass: Courtesy Margaret Glass

Photos of Calumet Farm: Main gate, cemetery (Barbara D. Livingston), office (Tom Hall)

Horse biographies: Nellie Flag (L.S. Sutcliffe from the Grayson collection), Bull Lea (Skeets Meadors), Whirlaway (The Blood-Horse), Mar-Kell (Skeets Meadors), Twilight Tear (World Wide Photos), Armed (The Blood-Horse), Citation (Skeets Meadors), Wistful (Skeets Meadors), Coaltown (Gulfstream Photo Service), Bewitch (Skeets Meadors), Real Delight (The Blood-Horse), Two Lea (The Blood-Horse), A Glitter (Bert Morgan), Tim Tam (Courier-Journal and Louisville Times), Forward Pass (Winants Bros.), Our Mims (NYRA/Joseph Farrington), Alydar (Milt Toby), Davona Dale (Dell Hancock), Before Dawn (Anne M. Eberhardt); Jones Boys with Bewitch, Armed, and Citation (The Blood-Horse).

Cover/book design by Brian Turner

Other Titles *from*
ECLIPSE PRESS

At the Wire
Horse Racing's Greatest Moments

Baffert
Dirt Road to the Derby

Cigar
America's Horse (revised edition)

Country Life Diary
(revised edition)

Crown Jewels of Thoroughbred Racing

Dynasties
Great Thoroughbred Stallions

Etched in Stone

Four Seasons of Racing

Great Horse Racing Mysteries

Hoofprints in the Sand
Wild Horses of the Atlantic Coast

Horse Racing's Holy Grail
The Epic Quest for the Kentucky Derby

Investing in Thoroughbreds
Strategies for Success

Lightning in a Jar
Catching Racing Fever

Matriarchs
Great Mares of the 20th Century

Olympic Equestrian

Ride of Their Lives
The Triumphs and Turmoils of Today's Top Jockeys

Royal Blood

Thoroughbred Champions
Top 100 Racehorses of the 20th Century

Women in Racing
In Their Own Words

THOROUGHBRED
Legends® SERIES

Affirmed and Alydar

Citation

Dr. Fager

Forego

Go for Wand

John Henry

Man o' War

Nashua

Native Dancer

Personal Ensign

Round Table

Ruffian

Seattle Slew

Spectacular Bid

Sunday Silence

Swaps

A Division of The Blood-Horse, Inc.
PUBLISHERS SINCE 1916